FRANCHISING IN JAPAN 2014

Legal and Business Considerations

KENDAL H. TYRE, JR., EXECUTIVE EDITOR
DIANA VILMENAY-HAMMOND, MANAGING EDITOR
PIERCE HAESUNG HAN, ASSISTANT EDITOR

LEXNOIR FOUNDATION

SECOND QUARTER 2014

LexNoir Foundation is the charitable, educational arm of LexNoir, an international network of lawyers connecting the African Diaspora.

This publication, *Franchising in Japan 2014: Legal and Business Considerations*, contains excerpts from *Franchising in Asia 2014: Legal and Business Considerations*. Both works are published by LexNoir Foundation and reflect the points of view of the authors and editors as of the date of publication and do not necessarily represent the opinions, interpretations, or positions of the law firms or organizations with which they are affiliated, nor the opinions, interpretations or positions of LexNoir Foundation or LexNoir.

Nothing contained in this book is to be considered as the rendering of legal advice, either generally or in connection with any specific issues or case. Readers are responsible for obtaining advice from their own legal counsel or other professional. This book, any forms and agreements or other information herein are intended for educational and informational purposes only.

www.lexnoir.org

Table of Contents

Franchising in Japan

Kakuji Mitani
Momo-o, Matsuo & Namba

Bibliography of International Franchise Resources

Kendal H. Tyre, Jr., Diana Vilmenay-Hammond, Pierce Haesung Han, Courtney L. Lindsay II and Keri McWilliams
Nixon Peabody LLP

Acknowledgment

This book could not have been written without the hard work and dedication of each of the contributing authors and editors. Thank you.

We would like to acknowledge and extend our heartfelt gratitude to Maria Stallings of the Washington, D.C. office of Nixon Peabody LLP for her invaluable assistance in revising, proofing, and editing this publication.

About the Editors and Authors

Kendal H. Tyre, Jr. – Kendal is a partner in the Washington, D.C. office of Nixon Peabody LLP. He handles domestic and cross-border transactions, including mergers and acquisitions, joint ventures, strategic alliances, licensing, and franchise matters.

In his franchise and licensing practice, Kendal counsels domestic and international franchisors, franchisees, licensors, licensees and distributors regarding U.S. state and federal franchise laws as well as foreign franchise legislation in a variety of jurisdictions. Kendal drafts and provides advice with regard to franchise and license agreements, disclosure documents and area development agreements and has extensive experience drafting and negotiating a variety of other commercial agreements. His client base spans the United States and foreign countries, including South Africa, Kenya, and the United Kingdom.

Kendal is a frequent contributor to franchise publications and a frequent speaker at franchise programs held by the American Bar Association Forum on Franchising and the International Franchise Association.

Kendal is co-chair of the firm's Diversity Action Committee and its Africa Group. Kendal is also the executive director of LexNoir Foundation.

E-mail address: ktyre@nixonpeabody.com

Diana Vilmenay-Hammond – Diana is an attorney in the Washington, D.C. office of Nixon Peabody LLP. She is a member of the firm's Franchise & Distribution team.

In her franchise practice, Diana works with domestic and international franchisors on transactional and litigation matters. Specifically, she counsels franchisor clients regarding state and federal franchise laws, disclosure and registration obligations. Diana drafts and negotiates various commercial agreements, including international franchise and development agreements.

Diana has co-authored numerous articles on franchising and frequently co-hosted the Nixon Peabody franchise law webinar series. Topics have included:

- "Franchise Case Law Round-Up: Implications for Your Franchise;"
- "Social Media Part II: Best Practices in Protecting Your Brand in the New Media;" and
- "The Awuah Case: Bellwether or Outlier."

Diana received her J.D. from Howard University School of Law and her B.A. from Georgetown University. She is a member of the American Bar Association (Forum on Franchising).

E-mail address: dvilmenay@nixonpeabody.com

Pierce Haesung Han – Pierce is an associate in Nixon Peabody's Global Business & Transactions group. Pierce focuses his practice on three main areas, assisting clients with a variety of complex business transactions.

- Mergers & Acquisitions: Providing assistance to both public and private clients with various mergers and acquisitions, performing due diligence, drafting and negotiating transaction documents, and facilitating closing and post-closing mechanics.
- International Commercial Transactions: Drafting and negotiating a variety of commercial agreements,

including international franchise and development agreements, license agreements, and purchase and sale agreements.

- Federal Securities Law Matters: Assisting public and private clients regarding federal securities laws and stock exchange rules relating to corporate governance and disclosure.

Pierce serves as the Secretary of the Asian Pacific Bar Association Educational Fund (an affiliate of the Asian Pacific American Bar Association of the Greater Washington, D.C. Area).

Pierce received his J.D. from Georgetown University Law Center and his B.A. from Case Western Reserve University. He is admitted to practice in the State of New York and the District of Columbia.

E-mail address: phan@nixonpeabody.com

Courtney L. Lindsay II – Courtney is an associate in Nixon Peabody's Corporate and Finance practice. In his corporate practice, Courtney assists for-profit and non-profit entities with transactional matters and corporate governance. In various capacities, Courtney has been involved in multiple merger and acquisition transactions, including drafting and managing due diligence.

Previously, Courtney worked in the legal and business affairs department at a national cable network, where he handled matters related to the network's LLC agreement, including drafting board and member consent agreements.

Courtney received his J.D. from the University of Virginia School of Law and his B.A. from the University of Virginia. He is admitted to practice in the Commonwealth of Virginia and the District of Columbia.

E-mail address: clindsay@nixonpeabody.com

Keri McWilliams – Keri is an associate in the Franchise & Distribution team of Nixon Peabody LLP. Keri works with clients on a number of franchising issues, including obtaining and maintaining franchise registrations in various states, responding to state inquiries regarding trade practices, ongoing compliance with state and federal regulations, and updating franchise disclosure documents. She also handles franchise sales counseling and franchise system issues.

Keri is a member of the American Bar Association's Forum on Franchising, and the Federal and Minnesota State bar associations. She is also a member of Minnesota Women Lawyers and the Minnesota Association of Black Lawyers, and a volunteer in the Volunteer Lawyers Network.

Keri received her J.D. from the Georgetown University Law Center and her B.F.A. from Washington University. She is admitted to practice in the District of Columbia and Minnesota.

E-mail address: kmcwilliams@nixonpeabody.com

Kakuji Mitani – Kakuji is a partner of Momo-o, Matsuo & Namba. He passed the Japanese National Bar Exam in 1999 and graduated from The University of Tokyo, Faculty of Law (LL.B.) in 2000. He then attended The Legal Training and Research Institute of the Supreme Court of Japan from 2001 to 2002 and was admitted to the Japanese Bar (The Dai-ichi Tokyo Bar Association in 2002). He began his career at Momo-o, Matsuo & Namba in 2002. In 2007, Kakuji graduated from Columbia University Law School with a Master of Laws degree and worked for Weil, Gotshal & Manges from 2007 to 2008. He was admitted to the New York Bar in 2008. Kakuji returned to Momo-o,

Matsuo & Namba in 2008 and became partner in 2011. Kakuji speaks Japanese and English.

E-mail address: mmn@mmn-law.gr.jp

About the Book

Franchising in Japan 2014: Legal and Business Considerations contains excerpts from the larger work *Franchising in Asia 2014: Legal and Business Considerations*. Both books serve as practical, succinct, easy-to-use reference tools for lawyers, business people and academics to use in navigating the laws and business issues impacting franchise arrangements in Asia.

This book provides an overview of the franchise industry in Japan and addresses the typical legal issues confronted when expanding a franchise system in Japan. The larger work, *Franchising in Asia 2014: Legal and Business Considerations*, covers those laws governing franchising in several other Asian countries.

In both books, an author, who is a legal expert in the designated jurisdiction, addresses the basic questions that a franchise lawyer would need to know to competently represent a client in expanding their franchise system to that country.

Each country chapter organizes a discussion of that country's laws under various headings and in a uniform format. Topics were sent to each country's author in the form of a questionnaire, and each author drafted responses to the questions presented. A general overview relating to the political and economic history of the country at the beginning of each chapter provides an initial context for the regulatory framework.[1]

---

[1]   The source of information for these sections is the Central Intelligence Agency,   https://www.cia.gov/library/publications/the-world-factbook/ (last visited May 15, 2014).

Apart from an overview of the legal framework for franchising, each book contains other articles and resources that should prove useful to those in the franchise industry.

The authors for each chapter are listed at the beginning of a chapter and their biographical information is listed in the previous section, *About the Editors and Authors.*

Readers should always consult with local counsel in the relevant jurisdiction instead of relying solely on the information contained in this book. The laws governing franchising are evolving and local counsel in Japan are best positioned to provide timely, relevant advice applying the current law to the particular facts of a case.

Franchising in Japan

Kakuji Mitani
Momo-o, Matsuo & Namba
Tokyo, Japan

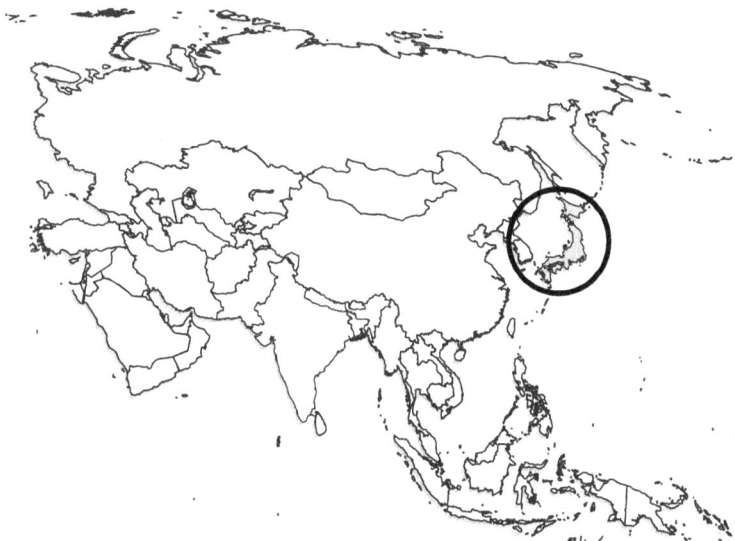

Japan

I.   Introduction

A.   Historical Background of the Country

After Japan's defeat in World War II, it recovered to become an economic power and an ally of the U.S. While the emperor retains his throne as a symbol of national unity, elected politicians hold actual decision-making power. Following three decades of unprecedented growth, Japan's economy experienced a major slowdown starting in the 1990s, but the country remains a major economic power. In March 2011, Japan's strongest-ever earthquake, and an accompanying tsunami, devastated the northeast part of Honshu island, killing thousands and damaging several nuclear power plants. The catastrophe had a negative impact on the country's economy and its energy infrastructure, and tested its ability to deal with humanitarian disasters.

B.   Economy of the Country

In the years following World War II, government-industry cooperation, a strong work ethic, mastery of high technology, and a comparatively small defense allocation (1% of GDP) helped Japan develop a technologically advanced economy. Two notable characteristics of the post-war economy were the close interlocking structures of manufacturers, suppliers, and distributors, known as *keiretsu*, and the guarantee of lifetime employment for a substantial portion of the urban labor force. Both features are now eroding under the dual pressures of global competition and domestic demographic change.

Japan's industrial sector is heavily dependent on imported raw materials and fuels. A tiny agricultural sector is highly subsidized and protected, with crop yields among the highest in the world. Usually self-sufficient in rice, Japan imports about 60% of its food on a caloric basis. Japan maintains one of the world's largest fishing fleets and accounts for nearly 15% of the global catch.

For three decades, overall real economic growth had been spectacular - a 10% average in the 1960s, a 5% average in the 1970s, and a 4% average in the 1980s. Growth slowed markedly in the 1990s, averaging just 1.7%, largely because of the after effects of inefficient investment and an asset price bubble in the late 1980s that required a protracted period of time for firms to reduce excess debt, capital, and labor. Modest economic growth continued after 2000, but the economy has fallen into recession three times since 2008.

A sharp downturn in business investment and global demand for Japan's exports in late 2008 pushed Japan into recession. Government stimulus spending helped the economy recover in late 2009 and 2010, but the economy contracted again in 2011 as the massive 9.0 magnitude earthquake in March disrupted manufacturing. Recovery spending helped boost GDP in early 2012, but slower global economic growth began weakening Japan's export-oriented economy by mid-year. Electricity supplies remain tight because Japan tentatively shut down almost all of its nuclear power plants after the Fukushima Daiichi nuclear reactors were crippled by the earthquake and resulting tsunami.

Newly-elected Prime Minister Shinzo Abe has declared the economy his government's top priority; he has pledged to reconsider his predecessor's plan to permanently close nuclear power plants and has said he will increase stimulus spending and press the Bank of Japan to loosen monetary policy. Measured on a purchasing power parity (PPP) basis that adjusts for price differences, Japan in 2012 stood as the fourth-largest economy in the world after second-place

Japan

China, which surpassed Japan in 2001, and third-place India, which edged out Japan in 2012. The new government will continue a longstanding debate on restructuring the economy and reining in Japan's huge government debt, which exceeds 200% of GDP. Persistent deflation, reliance on exports to drive growth, and an aging and shrinking population are other major long-term challenges for the economy.

C.   Franchise Legal Overview

Franchises are regulated as a "qualified chain-store business" under the *Small and Medium-sized Retail Business Promotion Act* ("**Act**"),[2] supplemented by the *Ministerial Order to Implement the Act* ("**Ministerial Order**"); concurrently, *Guidelines on Franchising under the Antimonopoly Act* ("**JFTC Guidelines**")[3] issued by Japan Fair Trade Commission (JFTC) are also applicable.[4]

---

[2]   The Act defines a "chain-store business" as "a business in which, according to standard contract, goods are continually sold, directly or by a designated third party, and assistance over the operation is continually given, principally to *medium- or small-sized* retailers." (Article 4.(5)) According to Article 2.(1) of the Act, a retailer is "*medium- or small-sized* if (a) its amount of the stated capital is 50 million yen or less, (b) the number of its permanent employees is 50 or less, or (c) it is an individual or a cooperative." The regulation set forth in the Act shall apply only to the transaction with such "medium- or small-sized" retailers.

[3]   The JFTC Guidelines are available online in English. See http://www.jftc.go.jp/en/legislation_gls/imonopoly_guidelines.files/franc hise.pdf (last visited May 15, 2014).

[4]   The JFTC Guidelines speculate as follows concerning the definition of "franchise system": "The franchise system is defined in many ways. However, the franchise system is generally considered to be a form of business in which the head office provides the member with the rights to use a specific trademark and trade name, and provides coordinated control, guidance, and support for the member's business and its management. The head office may provide support in relation to the selling of commodities and the provision of services. In return, the member pays the head office . . . . This document is intended for businesses that fit this definition and that have the characteristics

Japan

II.   Regulatory Requirements

A.   Pre-sale Disclosure

Please describe any pre-sale franchise disclosure or similar requirements that may apply to franchise transactions.

Under the Act, a franchisor is required to deliver a disclosure document before concluding a contract that falls into the category of "qualified chain-store business" with a franchisee.[5] The disclosure document shall include terms and conditions concerning the initial fee or development fee at the commencement of business, sales of goods/products by a franchisee, franchisor's management of business operation, trademark, store name, renewal and termination of the agreement, etc.

Further, the Ministerial Order sets forth the matters to be contained in a disclosure document in more detail. These include, for instance, the names of franchisor's directors, the number of franchisor's employees, franchisor's balance sheet and income statement for the past three years, the number of franchisees for the past three years, the number of lawsuits concerning the franchise agreement, non-competition obligation, the amount of penalties, etc.

---

mentioned . . . below, irrespective of what the business is called . . . . [1.(1)] The basis of the trading relationship for the franchise system is a franchise agreement between the head office and the member. This agreement is a standardized agreement that generally includes the following provisions: (a) A provision that grants the member permission to use the trademark and trade name of the head office; (b) A provision for the head office to provide the member with control and guidance to ensure there is a unified corporate identity for the business and to ensure that the member can maintain their business; (c) A provision for the member to pay the head office for the services mentioned in the previous two provisions; and (d) A provision concerning the termination of a franchise agreement." (1.(3))

[5]   Article 11.1

Japan

The Japan Franchise Association[6] ("**JFA**"), a trade association certified by the Ministry of Economy, Trade and Industry and comprised of major companies operating franchise businesses, has established voluntary principles and rules, although a franchisor is not required to join the JFA under the Act. As a practical matter, a major franchisor often submits to the JFA its disclosure document and obtains JFA's certification. The JFA's voluntary rule on disclosure requires that the prospective franchisee must be given seven days or more for consideration of the disclosure document before concluding the franchise agreement.

Concurrently, the JFTC Guidelines require a franchisor to disclose the information concerning its franchising system, including but not limited to, matters relating to the supply of products, the cost of guidance to a franchisee, royalties for the use of the trademark and trade name and for guidance in management, and loans extended to a franchisee. In addition, the JFTC Guidelines provide that, "from the viewpoint of the Antimonopoly Act," a disclosure document must be delivered sufficiently in advance so that the prospective franchisee can make an informed decision.[7]

B. Government Approvals, Registrations, Filing Requirements

Please describe any necessary government approvals, registrations, or filing requirements that may apply to franchise transactions.

---

[6]   http://www.jfa-fc.or.jp.e.ek.hp.transer.com/ (last visited May 15, 2014).

[7]   The JFTC Guidelines, Section 2.(2).A. *Editor's note*: As a practical matter, to comply with this voluntary rule it is recommended that the prospective franchisee be given seven days or more to review the disclosure document before executing the franchise agreement.

Japan

There are no legal requirements concerning government approvals, registrations or filings that may apply to franchise transactions. As a practical matter, however, a franchisor registers its disclosure document with the JFA and obtains the JFA's certification.

C. Limits on Fees and Typical Term of Franchise Agreement

Please describe any limits upon the nature and extent of fees and the term of a typical franchise agreement.

There is no specific restriction regarding the nature and extent of fees and the term of a franchise agreement under the franchise law. However, an excessively "unilateral" franchise agreement may be deemed in violation of the Antimonopoly Act as an unfair trade practice. The JFTC Guidelines provide that "when a franchise agreement or the actions of the head office [franchisor] are considered to exceed the boundaries for the conduct of proper business based on the franchise system, thereby providing the member [franchisee] with undue disadvantage regarding normal commercial practice, Item 14 (abuse of dominant bargaining position) of the General Designation[8] may be applied. In addition, where the restrictions placed on a member are illegal, Item 10 (Tie-in sale) or Item 13 (Dealing on restrictive terms) of the General Designation may be applied."[9] In terms of the JFTC Guidelines, a franchisor shall consider carefully the legality of the following conditions of the franchise agreement: (1) restriction on suppliers, (2) mandatory purchasing quotas,

---

[8]   "General Designation" is published by the JFTC as a category of an unfair trade practice under the Antimonopoly Act (Fair Trade Commission Public Notice No. 15 of June 18, 1982). See http://www.jftc.go.jp/en/legislation_gls/unfairtradepractices.html   (last visited May 15, 2014).

[9]   Id.

(3) restrictions on bargain sales, (4) revisions to the franchise agreement after it has been signed, (5) restrictions on trade after termination of an agreement, (6) tie-in sales and dealing on restrictive terms, and (7) restrictions on the sales price.

III.   Currency

If all payments under a franchise agreement must be made in immediately available U.S. Dollars, please advise as to any restrictions, reporting requirements, or regulations concerning the exchange, repatriation or remittance of U.S. Dollars.

There is no restriction on the payment under a franchise agreement being made in U.S. Dollars. If the payment (both inbound and outbound) exceeds certain thresholds under the Foreign Exchange and Foreign Trade Control Act, a party is required to report it to the Bank of Japan.

IV.   Taxes, Tariffs, and Duties

Please do not provide any in-depth comments on tax structuring. However, please provide your general comments on the typical amount of withholding tax that would apply and whether a "gross-up" provision contained in a franchise agreement would be enforceable in your country.

A withholding tax of 20% will be imposed on royalties paid to non-residents or foreign entities pursuant to the Income Tax Act, in principle. However, Japan has a double taxation treaty with more than sixty countries, including the United States, and a withholding tax is exempted or reduced depending upon such treaty. The exemption may be obtained on an application-basis to the competent Japanese tax authority.

The "gross-up" provision is enforceable in Japan, in principle. Please take notice that the "gross-up" provision may affect the total amount to be paid by a franchisee to a franchisor, and therefore a franchisor is required to explain the impact of the provision very carefully and let a franchisee fully understand it, or the provision will possibly be declared invalid by courts in Japan.

V.   Trademarks

Please advise us as to whether there are any special requirements for granting a valid trademark license, including the use of a registered user agreement or a short trademark license agreement and any required filing of such an agreement with the trademark authorities.

There are no special requirements for granting a valid trademark license in Japan,[10] although it is very important for a franchisor to register its trademark(s) at the Patent Office before entering into the market because Japan adopts the registration principle (first-to-file rule) under the Trademark Act. As long as certain criteria are met, the trademark can be registered even if the trademark is not currently in use, while the registered trademark is broadly protected under the Trademark Act.

The license of the registered trademark is usually a part of the franchise agreement. Thus, a franchisor must register its trademark(s) at the Patent Office in order to exercise its trademark rights. If the same or similar trademark is already registered by a third party at the Patent Office, the

---

[10]   The license agreement is not required to be registered, but an exclusive license can be registered under the Trademark Act. If there is a registration of an exclusive license, a trademark owner is not able to exercise the right as a trademark owner, unless such registration has expired. Practically speaking, the registration of an exclusive license is not common.

use of the trademark could be prohibited by an injunctive order claimed by the trademark owner.

VI. Restrictions on Transfer

Please advise as to whether there are any restrictions (1) on a franchisor to restrict transfers by a master franchisee, any interest in a master franchisee, or the assets of the master franchisee or (2) the ability of a master franchisee to control and/or restrict transfers of a subfranchisee's rights under a master franchise agreement, interest in the subfranchisee, or the assets of the subfranchisee.

There are no special provisions regarding transfer of the franchise agreement. However, in the event that the provision proscribing such transfer is unreasonably and unilaterally in favor of a franchisor and against the public order and morality under the Civil Law of Japan, the provision will be deemed invalid by courts in Japan. The JFTC could also consider the provision against the JFTC Guidelines.

VII. Termination

Please advise us as to any laws relating to termination in your country, such as agency laws, required indemnity provisions, notice or "good cause" requirements, or other laws affecting termination of a franchise agreement. Please describe.

There are no special provisions regarding the termination of the franchise agreement; provided, however, the terms and conditions concerning termination must be fully explained to the franchisee before the signing of the agreement under the Act.

In addition, as well as the transfer provision above, in the event that the provision concerning the termination is unreasonably and unilaterally in favor of a franchisor and against the public order and morality under the Civil Law, the provision will be deemed invalid by courts in Japan. As well, the JFTC could consider the provision against the JFTC Guidelines.

Further, it should be noted that, as a general rule, when two parties are in a continuous relationship of distribution, court precedents in Japan tend to protect the interests of the terminated party, and to restrict the right of the terminating party to terminate the contract, without any notice or compensation, provided that the terminated party has not breached the contract or has not acted in bad faith. Thus, if a franchisor intends to terminate the agreement, caution should be exercised and the franchisor should act in full compliance with the procedures set forth in the agreement.

VIII. Governing Law, Jurisdiction, and Dispute Resolution

A.   Choice of Law of Foreign Jurisdiction

Please confirm whether the choice of law of a foreign jurisdiction would likely to be upheld under the law of the country, except for certain matters such as trademarks, bankruptcy and competition matters, which we assume would be governed by the law in your country.

Under the Act on General Rules for Application of Laws, the parties may select the governing law at the conclusion of the agreement.[11]

---

[11]   Article 7 stipulates as follows: "The formation and effect of a juridical act shall be governed by the law of the place chosen by the parties at the time of the act."

Japan

B. International Arbitration Dispute Resolution

Please confirm that a court in your country would honor an election of international arbitration dispute resolution, and therefore refuse to hear any disputes arising under a franchise agreement.

If the franchise agreement contains a provision under which any dispute shall be resolved by arbitration, a court in Japan is required to dismiss a filed lawsuit under the Arbitration Act.[12] Japan is a signatory to the *Convention on the Recognition and Enforcement of Foreign Arbitral Awards* (the "New York Convention").

IX. Non-Competition Provisions

If the franchise agreement prohibits the franchisee from engaging in certain competitive activities during the term of the agreement, and for a 12-month period after the termination or expiration of the agreement, please comment on the enforceability of non-competition covenants in your country.

A non-competition provision in a franchise agreement is generally permitted in terms of the purpose of the franchise system; provided, however, that unreasonable restrictions on the franchisee's business might be deemed illegal by the JFTC under the Antimonopoly Act.

---

[12] Article 14. Provided, however, that this principle shall not apply (i) when the arbitration agreement is null and void, cancelled, or for other reasons invalid; (ii) when arbitration proceedings are inoperative or incapable of being performed based on the arbitration agreement; or (iii) when the request is made by the defendant subsequent to the presentation of its statement in the oral hearing or in the preparations for argument proceedings on the substance of the dispute. Id.

As for non-competition obligations of a franchisee after the termination, the JFTC Guidelines stipulate that the obligations that are not necessary to protect its franchise business or know-how may violate the Antimonopoly Act. Although it depends on each case, as a general rule, a 12-month period after the termination of the agreement may be considered reasonable under current business conditions.

X.   Language Requirements

Does the law in your country require that a franchise agreement be translated into the local language in order to be enforceable between the parties?

The Act provides no requirement on the language used for the disclosure documents or franchise agreement, nor is a language requirement explicitly mentioned in the JFTC Guidelines.

Thus, there is no legal limitation on the disclosure to a potential franchisee being made in a foreign language. However, the disclosure must be fully understood by a franchisee under the Act and the JFTC Guidelines. As a practical matter, a disclosure document and a franchise agreement is prepared in Japanese for a franchisee's understanding.

XI.   Other Significant Matters

Please advise as to whether there are any significant matters not addressed above of which a franchisor should be aware in connection with its entering into a franchise agreement in your country.

Although there is no legal requirement that a franchisor must become a member of the official franchise trade association, the JFA, many major franchisors and

Japan

franchisees are JFA members. The JFA reviews disclosure documents and certifies their creation in accordance with the Act. The JFA operates the website *"The Franchise"*[13] for a franchisee, where disclosure documents of major franchisors, including but not limited to 7-Eleven Japan, McDonald's Japan, and 31 Ice Cream (Baskin-Robbins), are available to the public.

---

[13]   http://frn.jfa-fc.or.jp/ (Japanese only) (last visited May 15, 2014).

Bibliography of International Franchise Resources

*Kendal H. Tyre, Jr., Diana Vilmenay-Hammond,
Pierce Haesung Han, Courtney L. Lindsay II and
Keri McWilliams*
Nixon Peabody LLP
Washington, D.C.

I.　General International Resources

Mark Abell, Gary R. Duvall, and Andrea Oricchio Kirsh, *International Franchise Legislation* B1, ABA FORUM ON FRANCHISING (1996)

Kathleen C. Anderson and Anthony M. Stiegler, *Put Muscle in Your Marks: Enforcing Intellectual Property Rights* W14, ABA FORUM ON FRANCHISING (1995)

Richard M. Asbill and Jane W. LaFranchi, *International Franchise Sales Laws—A Survey* W7, ABA FORUM ON FRANCHISING (2005)

Jeffery A. Brimer, Alison C. McElroy, and John Pratt, *Going International: What Additional Restraints Will You Face?* W4, ABA FORUM ON FRANCHISING (2011)

Michael G. Brennan, Alexander Konigsberg, and Philip F. Zeidman, *Globetrotting: A Workshop on International Franchising* 10/W8, ABA FORUM ON FRANCHISING (1994)

Michael G. Brennan, Alexander Konigsberg, and Philip F. Zeidman, *Globetrotting: Strategies for Launching U.S. Franchisors Abroad* 2/P2, ABA FORUM ON FRANCHISING (1994)

Christopher P. Bussert and Jennifer Dolman, *Regaining Your Trademark After Abandonment or Misappropriation* W7, ABA FORUM ON FRANCHISING (2011)

Ronald T. Coleman and Linda K. Stevens, *Trade Secrets and Confidential Information: Rights and Remedies* W2, ABA FORUM ON FRANCHISING (2000)

Finola Cunningham, *Commerce Department Helps Franchisors Go Global*, in FRANCHISING WORLD 63 (Dec. 2005)

Michael R. Daigle and Alex S. Konigsberg, *Meeting Off-Shore Disclosure and Contract Requirements* F/W13, ABA FORUM ON FRANCHISING (1992)

Jennifer Dolman, Robert A. Lauer, and Lawrence M. Weinberg, Structuring International Master Franchise Relationships for Success and Responding When Things Go Awry W22, ABA FORUM ON FRANCHISING (2007)

Gary R. Duvall, Paul Jones, and Jane LaFranchi, *Planning for the International Enforcement of Franchise Agreements* W6, ABA FORUM ON FRANCHISING (1999)

William Edwards, International Expansion: Do Opportunities Outweigh Challenges? in FRANCHISING WORLD (February 2008)

George J. Eydt and Stuart Hershman, *Bringing a Foreign Franchise System to the United States* W9, ABA FORUM ON FRANCHISING (2009)

William A. Finkelstein and Louis T. Pirkey, *International Trademarks* W15, ABA FORUM ON FRANCHISING (1991)

William A. Finkelstein, Protecting Trademarks Internationally: Current Strategies and Developments B3, ABA FORUM ON FRANCHISING (1996)

Stephen Giles, Lou H. Jones, and Lawrence Weinberg, *Negotiating and Documenting Complex International Franchise Agreements* W21, ABA FORUM ON FRANCHISING (2006)

Steven M. Goldman, Stephen Giles, Marc Israel, and Stanley Wong, *Competition Round Up from Around the World* LB2, ABA FORUM ON FRANCHISING (2004)

David C. Gryce and E. Lynn Perry, *Trademarks and Copyrights in the International Arena* 6/W4, ABA FORUM ON FRANCHISING (1993)

Kenneth S. Kaplan, Andrew P. Loewinger, and Penelope J. Ward, *System Standards in International Franchising* W14, ABA FORUM ON FRANCHISING (2005)

Edward Levitt and Jorge Mondragon, A Survey of International Legal Traps and How to Avoid Them—Beyond the Franchise Laws W20, ABA FORUM ON FRANCHISING (2007)

Ned Levitt, Kendal H. Tyre, and Penny Ward, *The Impossible Dream: Controlling Your International Franchise System* W4, ABA FORUM ON FRANCHISING (2010)

Michael K. Lindsey and Andrew P. Loewinger, *International (Non-U.S.) Franchise Disclosure Requirements* W9, ABA FORUM ON FRANCHISING (2002)

Andrew P. Loewinger and John Pratt, *Recent Changes and Trends in International Franchise Laws* W4, ABA FORUM ON FRANCHISING (2008)

Andrew P. Loewinger and Thomas M. Pitegoff, Avoiding the Long Arm of the Law in International Franchising: Issues and Approaches W8, ABA FORUM ON FRANCHISING (1995)

Craig J. Madson and Katherine C. Spelman, *Similarity and Confusion in the Intellectual Property Arena* W11, ABA FORUM ON FRANCHISING (1997)

Christopher A. Nowak, John Pratt, and Carl E. Zwisler, *Franchising Internationally with Countries with Opaque Legal Systems* W20, ABA FORUM ON FRANCHISING (2006)

E. Lynn Perry and John L. Sullivan Jr., *Trademark Compliance and Enforcement Techniques* E/W12, ABA FORUM ON FRANCHISING (1992)

Marcel Portmann, *Franchising Sector Proves Global Reach*, in FRANCHISING WORLD (January 2007)

John Pratt and Luiz Henrique O. do Amaral, Civil Law for Common Law Practitioners (or How to Draft an Agreement for Use Overseas) W4, ABA FORUM ON FRANCHISING (2002)

Kirk W. Reilly, Robert F. Salkowski and Geoffrey B. Shaw, *Determining the Rules of Engagement in Litigation Here and Abroad* W5, ABA FORUM ON FRANCHISING (2008)

Catherine Riesterer and Frank Zaid, *Basics of International Franchising* L/B2, ABA FORUM ON FRANCHISING (1997)

W. Andrew Scott and Christopher N. Wormald, *Stranger in a Strange Land: Contrasting Franchising in International Expansion* W2, ABA FORUM ON FRANCHISING (2003)

Donald Smith and Erik Wulff, *International Franchising: The Unraveling of an International Franchise Relationship* 15/W13, ABA FORUM ON FRANCHISING (1993)

Frank Zaid, Pamela Mills, and Michael Santa Maria, *Essential Issues in International Franchising* LB/1, ABA FORUM ON FRANCHISING (2001)

II.   Asian Resources

Stephen Giles, Andrew P. Loewinger, and Sherin Sakr, *Go East Young Franchisor: Franchising in Asia-Pacific Other Than China and India* W21, ABA FORUM ON FRANCHISING (2011)

Stephen Giles, *Franchising in Asia-Pacific Region, Who's Who Legal*: FRANCHISE 2012 (2012)

A.   China

Ren Yanling, *Changes to Chinese Franchise Law: An improved Balance Between the Interests of Franchisors and Franchisees*, in INT'L JOURNAL OF FRANCHISING LAW 3 (2012)

China: New Franchsing Law, in Int'l Journal of FRANCHISING LAW 2 (2005)

Ella S.K. Cheong, *China*, in INTERNATIONAL FRANCHISING CHN/1 (Dennis Campbell gen. ed. 2011)

Yu Qin and Richard L. Wageman, *China*, in INTERNATIONAL FRANCHISE SALES LAWS China-1 (Andrew P. Loewinger and Michael K. Lindsey eds. 2010)

Mark Abell, Daniela C. Brito, and Paul D. Jones, *Franchising in the BRIC Markets (Brazil, Russia, India, and China)* W18, ABA FORUM ON FRANCHISING (2008)

B.   Hong Kong

Andrea S.Y. Fong, *Hong Kong*, in INTERNATIONAL FRANCHISING HK/1 (Dennis Campbell gen. ed. 2011)

C.   India

Preeti Mehta, *India—Termination of Master Franchise Agreements and the Consequences*, in INT'L JOURNAL OF FRANCHISING LAW 3 (2007)

Yoginder Pal, *Franchising in India*, FRANCHISING WORLD (October 2006)

Mark Abell, Daniela C. Brito and Paul D. Jones, *Franchising in the BRIC Markets (Brazil, Russia, India, and China)* W18, ABA FORUM ON FRANCHISING (2008)

D.   Indonesia

Sigit Ardianto and Rivan F. Ramadhan, *Indonesia*, in INTERNATIONAL FRANCHISING INA/1 (Dennis Campbell gen. ed. 2011)

Rick Beckman and Ferry P. Madian, *Indonesia*, in INTERNATIONAL FRANCHISE SALES LAWS Indonesia-1 (Andrew P. Loewinger and Michael K. Lindsey eds. 2010)

Kendal H. Tyre, Jr. & Pierce Haesung Han, *The Ministry of Trade of Indonesia Limits Growth of Food and Beverage*

Franchises, NIXON PEABODY LLP: FRANCHISE ALERT (February 2013)

E.   Japan

Takenari Shimizu, *Japan*, in INTERNATIONAL FRANCHISING JAP/1 (Dennis Campbell gen. ed. 2011)

Souichirou Kozuka and Takashi Kanai, *Japan*, in INTERNATIONAL FRANCHISE SALES LAWS Japan-1 (Andrew P. Loewinger and Michael K. Lindsey eds. 2010)

F.   Malaysia

Leela Baskaran, *Malaysia*, in INTERNATIONAL FRANCHISING MAY/1 (Dennis Campbell gen. ed. 2011)

Mohd Bustaman Hj Abdullah and Wong Sai Fong, *Malaysia*, in INTERNATIONAL FRANCHISE SALES LAWS Malaysia-1 (Andrew P. Loewinger and Michael K. Lindsey eds. 2010)

Kendal H. Tyre, Jr. & Pierce Haesung Han, *Malaysian Government Actively Promotes Growth in Franchise Sector*, NIXON PEABODY LLP: FRANCHISE ALERT (October 2013)

G.   Singapore

Daniel Lim, Bernard Lui, Michele The, and Vanessa Chew, *Singapore*, in INTERNATIONAL FRANCHISING SIN/1 (Dennis Campbell gen. ed. 2011)

H.   South Korea

Brendon Carr and Jae-Hoon Kim, *South Korea*, in INTERNATIONAL FRANCHISE SALES LAWS South Korea-1 (Andrew P. Loewinger and Michael K. Lindsey eds. 2010)

I. Taiwan

Wellington Liu and David Lu, *Taiwan*, in INTERNATIONAL FRANCHISE SALES LAWS Taiwan-1 (Andrew P. Loewinger and Michael K. Lindsey eds. 2010)

J. Thailand

Alan Adcock and Sriwan Puapondh, *Thailand*, in INTERNATIONAL FRANCHISING THA/1 (Dennis Campbell gen. ed. 2011)

K. Vietnam

Mai Minh Hang and Nguyen Anh Tran, *Vietnam*, in INTERNATIONAL FRANCHISE SALES LAWS Vietnam-1 (Andrew P. Loewinger and Michael K. Lindsey eds. 2010)